Jake Parker

# NUTHIN' BUT MECH 2

sketches and renderings

Nuthin' But Mech 2
Copyright ©2014 by Design Studio Press

Graphic Design: Cecilia Zo
Art Direction: Scott Robertson
Copy Editing: Jessica Hoffmann


Published by
Design Studio Press
8577 Higuera Street
Culver City, CA 90232


www.designstudiopress.com
info@designstudiopress.com


10 9 8 7 6 5 4 3 2 1
Printed in China
First edition, June 2014

Paperback ISBN
978-162465010-9

Library of Congress Control Number 2013922214

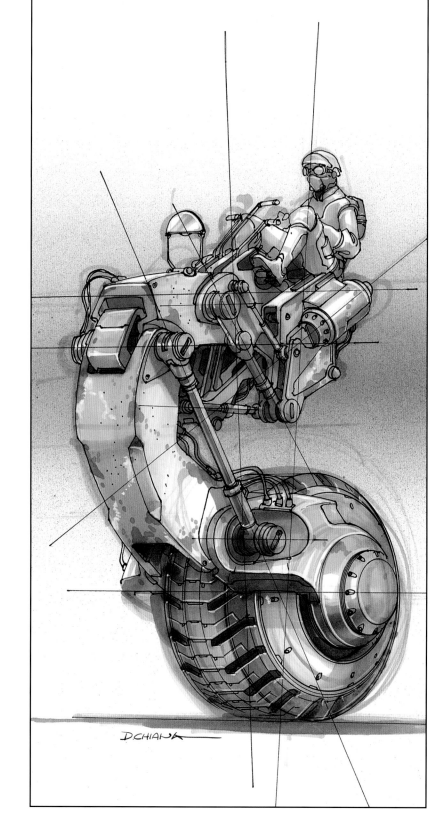

**FRONT COVER IMAGE:** *(left to right)*
Colie Wertz, Chris Stoski, Francis Tsai, and
Eric Joyner

**BACK COVER IMAGE:** Doug Chiang

Cover typeset in Orbitron, designed by
Matt McInerney


Book typeset in Fedra Sans and Rotis

# Contents

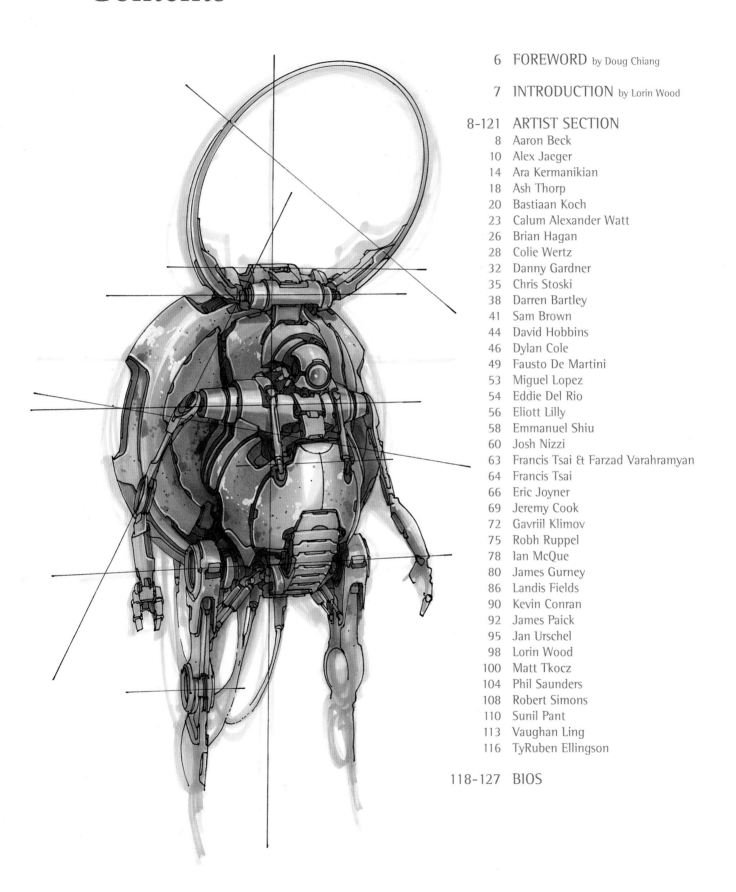

# Foreword

Machines. Robots. Mechs. Although it may seem that mechs are a modern invention, they have in fact appeared in stories since ancient times. In Greek mythology, the god Hephaestus built mechanical servants. The statue of Galatea from Pygmalion, Talos the bronze giant that protected Crete, and the clay golems of Jewish folklore were all mechs. The earliest practical mechs, complex self-operating machines called automata, were first conceived of in the 13th century. Leonardo da Vinci designed his own in 1495. And by the 17th century, Japan and France had built functioning automata.

Nuthin' But Mech celebrates this rich heritage of mech design and invention with work by some of the leading artists and designers in entertainment today. These visionaries have fashioned mechanical marvels worthy of their legendary predecessors.

As a production designer and concept artist, nothing excites me more than watching blank canvases be magically transformed into brilliant mechanical designs. With 2-D and 3-D rendering techniques, incredibly rich and exotic imagery is now possible. Although you can realize almost anything you can imagine, the key is still deciding what to do and then doing it well.

But what makes for a great mech design? The secret lies in the joints, the junction between 2 forms that provides the pivot point for motion. How a joint is expressed in shape and form determines the success and beauty of a mech design. By combining the six simple machine types—wheel, lever, inclined plane, wedge, and screw—these artists have devised elaborate and ingenious mechs that are as diverse as their creators.

I marvel at the skill and imagination demonstrated in these pieces. Not only is the sophistication of the designs apparent, but so are the stories behind each image. These artists are more than accomplished painters, designers, engineers, and scientists; they are also storytellers. Drawing beautiful images means little without context. And the worlds dreamt up by these creators give life to their creations.

*Nuthin' But Mech* is nothing but amazing.


*D.CHIANG*

Doug Chiang

# Introduction

Once again we find ourselves immersed in a world of highly imaginative mechanoids of every shape and size. After the success of the first *Nuthin' But Mech* book, Scott Robertson graciously afforded me an opportunity to continue this journey and gather the next batch of incredibly talented artists. A healthy portion were invited to contribute based on their excitement about the first book, and it was my pleasure to add their work to this opus of ephemeral decadence. I also wanted to include some illustrators who continue to hold down the fort of analog media: James Gurney (creator of *Dinotopia*) and Eric Joyner (who holds the market on robots and donuts).

As with the previous volume, when the work came flooding in, I was continuing to alter and question my own pieces for the book. It was literally a visual-stimulus overload. Being among some of the masters was once again a massive honor, which I now pass along to you.

I would also like to note that this is a very special volume. When publishing with this number of artists, the proceeds are generally donated to a charity that we collectively choose. I am extremely proud and honored that the contributors have decided to donate the royalties to an inspiring individual who also happens to be one of the artists in this book: Francis Tsai. When we began working on the first Nuthin' But Mech, Francis was one of the first to jump on board, but he soon informed Scott and me that he had been diagnosed with Amyotrophic Lateral Sclerosis (ALS), or Lou Gehrig's disease. This affliction quickly took from him the basic motor skills that he had depended upon as a conceptual artist. Despite this traumatic event, he has persisted in his craft with the aid of an amazing piece of technology that tracks his eye movements and translates them to his desktop software. His friends and family, especially his amazing wife, Linda, continue to support and encourage Francis, which in turn inspired each of us who contributed. We felt this was a more worthy cause for the proceeds.

To learn more about Francis, I encourage you to visit his studio webpage at http://teamgt.com.

Managing an undertaking like this is no small task, but I honestly never felt the full pressure that I should have. The caliber of work, passion, and generosity of each of these artists made this project an absolute joy to be part of. I hope that as you flip through these pages, you will be as creatively edified and inspired as I have been fortunate enough to be...twice.

Welcome back to the world of *Nuthin' But Mech!*

Lorin Wood
August 2013
Dallas, Texas

Aaron Beck

# Alex Jaeger

Even after the success of the FRS-32R last year, we've continued to make improvements. The newest addition to JAEGERTECH's racing division is the all-new FRS-XX. With a 6-leg chassis and lighter construction, it continues to dominate the W.M.R.C. in all venues.

As part of the TR series, the S.A.R.X. is a specialized drone mech designed to tread into hazardous locations and crawl into tunnels and vertical shafts without a tether. Armed with powerful mapping technologies, it can help save lives and prevent injuries during search-and-rescue efforts.

# Ara Kermanikian

Excerpted from a story I am working on:

After centuries of brutal wars, the 2 superpowers agreed to a truce. All of their conflicts were now resolved through an annual air duel. They all agreed to, at worst, sacrifice the lives of 1 or 2 pilots a year instead of the millions in prior wars. It was a great honor for the pilots, who were trained from childhood for the duels; they were celebrities and heroes. Deciding the outcome of conflicts with a duel worked well for a couple of decades, and then, as things always do, the process became corrupt. The duels started to get rigged by industrialists, barons, banks, and politicians.

The Goliath mech program was a joint initiative to create a defense war machine that would help keep the peace and protect the populations of both sides from possible external or internal threats. 7,000 mechs were manufactured and were about to be delivered. Each side was to get 3,000, and the rest would be kept as backups or harvested for parts during the mechs' 1,000-year lifetime. Each mech needed 3 pilots: a driver, a weapons expert, and a navigator. Each mech was also accompanied by a drone, which was its transport as well as its aerial support and reconnaissance.

The superstar pilot of the last duel, refusing to take a dive, discovered that his fighter had been tampered with to ensure his loss. Using the tampering to his advantage, he managed to defeat his opponent and upset the underground agreements, the biggest of which was the wager of the entirety of one side's balance for the manufacture of their mechs. Knowing that the debt would crush their economy, the losing side decided to nationalize all 7,000 mechs and mount a war using them to annihilate the other side.

The story continues...

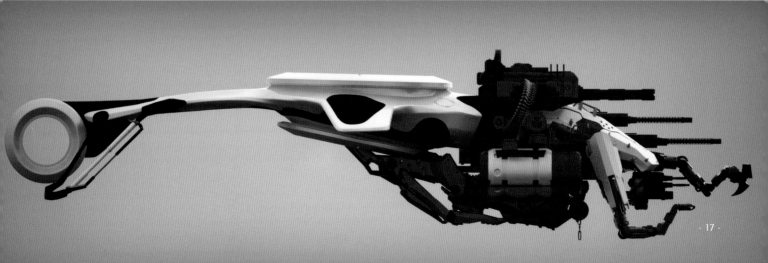

Ash Thorp

失われた少年

Bastiaan Koch

IMMUTECH
ROBOTICS.COM
BA

Calum Alexander Watt

Brian Hagan

# Colie Wertz

# hypercesta

# ballistix

**ACCELERATED PRODUCTS FOR A FASTER AGE.**

HYPERCESTA

Danny Gardner

# Darren Bartley

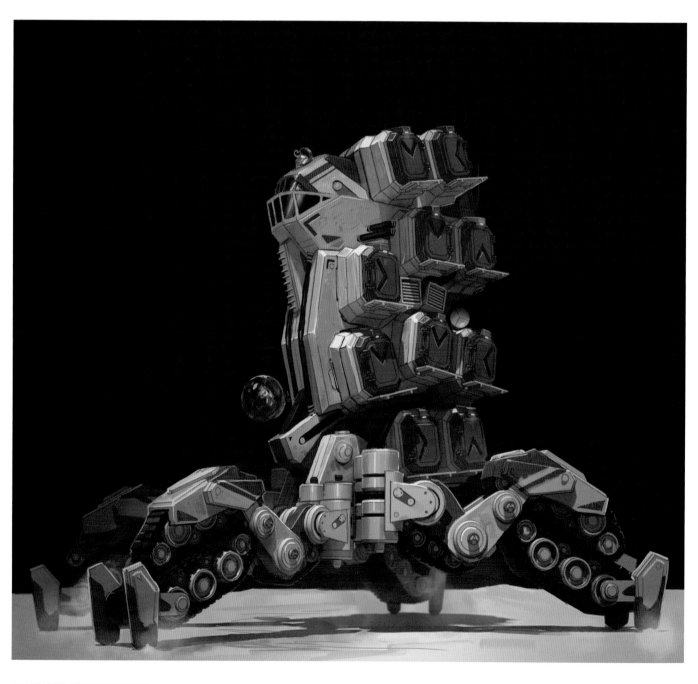

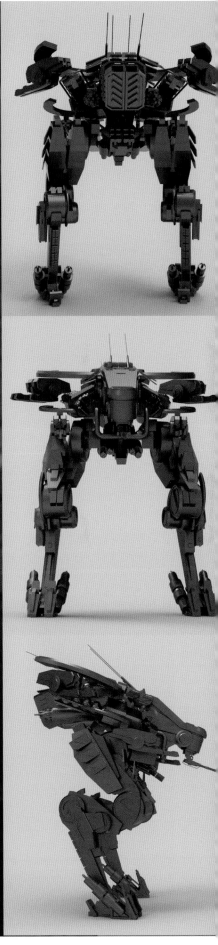

Sam Brown

# Dylan Cole

For my piece, I wanted to do something a little different. Lately I have been enjoying a lot of old sci-fi: *Flash Gordon*, *Buck Rogers*, etc. So I wanted to take the aesthetic of those old spaceships and apply it to a mech. In addition to the mech design, I also wanted the old pulp art to influence my palette and composition. To me that meant red, cyan, and cream and a more formal composition. I had a blast with this piece. It was fun to finally do a painting in the genre that I have loved for so long.

→ right
Retro Red Mech Sketch

This was my first sketch. The basic design of the mechs and the composition did not change very much. When I do sketches like this for myself, I don't put much style into them; they are strictly informative for composition. I find it easy to be seduced by the textural brushes, so I just use a lot of the simple lasso tool and big-brush painting.

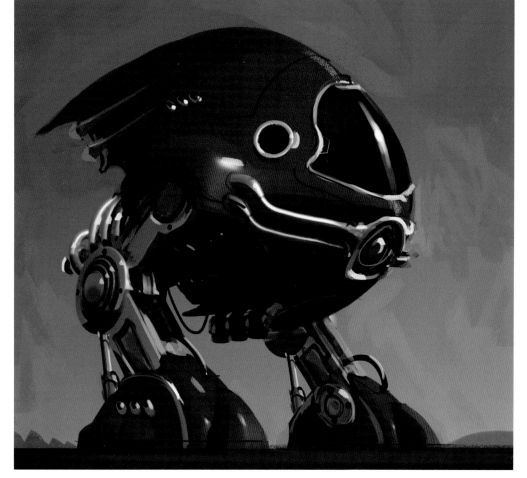

← left
Retro Red Mech Alternate Design

As I am modeling, I often do a quick render and then paint over it to work on design details. I find it a lot quicker to work out design ideas in 2-D. This was an alternate design idea that lost the pointy nose for some sort of intake. I was extremely conflicted about this. This version might work better as a mech design, but I just couldn't stand to lose the classic pointy nose from the old spaceships.

↑ above
Retro Red Mech Model

Here is a screen grab of the model in Cinema 4D before rendering. I only modeled what detail I thought was necessary, since I knew I would be doing a lot of the detail in Photoshop.

↑ above
Retro Red Mech Render

This is an assembly of all the final render passes. You can see that there are no cut lines or smaller details. In addition to these passes, I also rendered out fully chrome versions so that I could mix in additional chrome details. You can see examples of this on the tail and on the trim of the main body.

↓ next page
Retro Red Mech Final Design

To finish it up, I used a lot of matte painting techniques to create the sky and landscape. I modeled some simple alien plants and created a blobby shader with a lot of displacement. I rendered these out in several angles and configurations and used those to populate the ground. I added all the details to the mech with digital paint and paths. The behind-the-scenes pic you are not seeing is me wearing white long underwear with Halloween pirate boots in my backyard. However, it did the job, and with some serious paintwork, I had my classic space hero. I reluctantly lost the bubble space helmet from my sketch because I liked the pose of him shielding his eyes.

Fausto De Martini

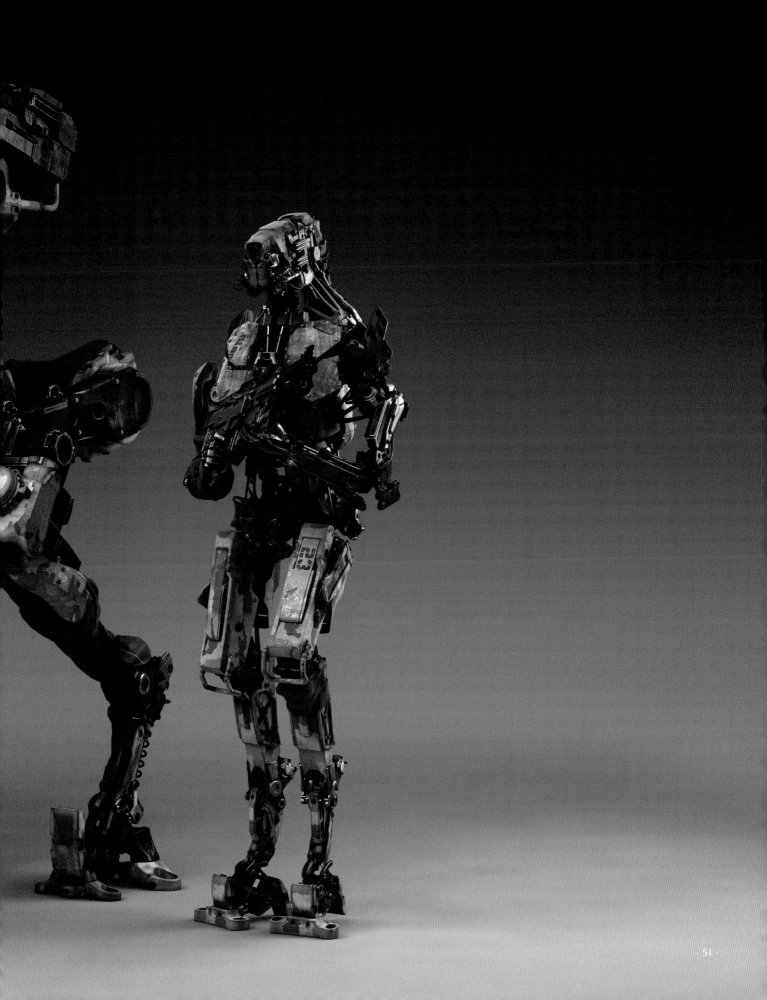

Miguel Lopez

Eddie Del Rio

Del Rio

Del Rio

Eliott Lilly

# IRON FIST LOSES!
## DESTROYED BY HORRID 'REAPRS IN WORLD RECORD TIME.

# FINDING THE GIANT

**Photograph by Emmanuel Shiu, June, 2020**

This is the stuff of legend. When we first heard of the Giant, no one could believe it. We are referring to the 200 foot tall World War 2 gigantic robot, Russia's answer to the nuclear bomb. Even though there were sketches and blueprints found many years ago (right), it was always a myth – an urban legend. But when a salvage team stumbled upon a base on their survey mission in the Kuril Trench, it was a myth no more. The scientists are still trying to figure out what exactly happened here. Robot parts (above) are strewn about the ocean floor on the way to the base, suggesting some type of explosion to the base. The bigger question is: how were the Russians intending to use this robot? As the submersibles enter the base, an eerie silhouette of a huge mechanical being can be seen. There are no other words to describe this, so we gave it the most appropriate name we could – **The Giant.**

Emmanuel Shiu

*The Subs surveys the wreckage, June, 2020*

# Josh Nizzi

Power Armor

Hacked together with parts from other robots and vehicles, this power armor isn't pretty, but it packs a mean punch. Its weapons include 3 Gatling guns, a flamethrower, and a shotgun. The pilot rides in style with a cockpit made from a classic motorcycle.

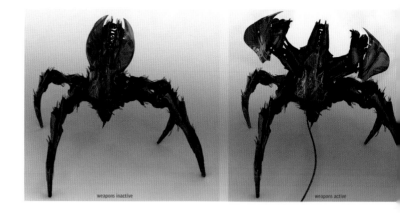

weapons inactive · weapons active

↓ below

Tic

These creepy bots were built for stealth recon in the outer limits of colonized space. They are loaded with multiple sensors and various communications equipment. If needed, they can deploy a hyper-dexterous tentacle to manipulate objects or spy in places their body will not fit.

↑ above

Modes

If threatened, the bot goes into battle mode, revealing dual plasma guns.

right→

Tic Scale

These bots are large enough to be a deadly threat to anybody without serious firepower.

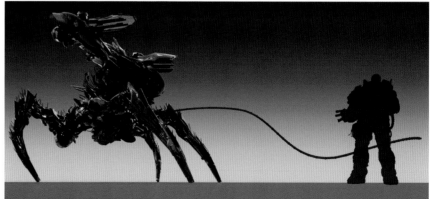

Francis Tsai & Farzad Varahramyan

Francis Tsai

# Eric Joyner

Jeremy Cook

Gavriil Klimov

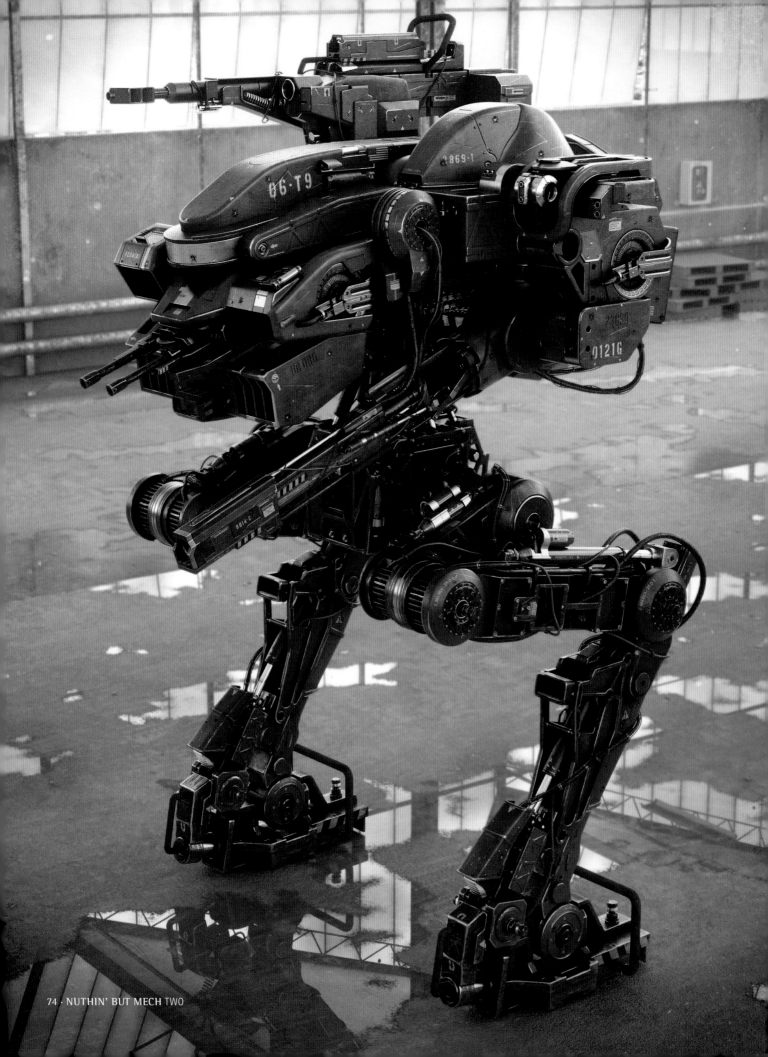

Robh Ruppel

Ian McQue

# James Gurney

Poseidon D-class bronto strutters require frequent fluid-exchange service. Drainage men, stationed at remote outposts along the steam safari routes of the Great Desert, replace hydraulic oil from the quad pistons after every 50,000 cycles. They also check lube levels, and they pump water into the belly tanks for the long hauls.

This is one of Dinotopia's mothballed mech dinosaurs, called "strutters," that Arthur Denison found in the caves beneath the island. He narrowly escapes from a T. rex, who bites off the Ceratopsian head/windshield. The passenger seat is built into the flanges of the pelvis, and the driver's seat is between the scapulas. The greebles alongside the back leg include the actuators, governors, valves, meters, and lube points. The rendering is in oil, based on a kit-bashed reference model, cobbled together from random parts of old Japanese robots and jet fighters.

↖ left up
Grapple Hold

Spade Sorgoff's armada-class strutter takes down a tyrannosaur at the Battle of the Backbone Mountains. The armada strutters and the mantis-class mech walkers from Dinotopia's Age of Heroes are modeled on the body plan of Carboniferous invertebrates. They lead the northern assault on the Rainy Basin, overcoming scattered rebels guarding the carnosaur's domain.

↙ left down
Emissary

Hohepa, astride his tyrannosaur, wades across the shallows of Buckthorn Creek to parley with an invading force of shield strutters. His action prevents the destruction of the hatchery at Moss Valley, but leads to the Armakians breaking off their alliance. Hohepa later becomes the mentor of Blake Terrapin.

↑ above
Strutter Downshot, oil on board, 14 x 28 inches

These Dinotopian strutters were discovered by Arthur Denison and Lee Crabb, who reengaged the sunstone-steamer engines. Ancient Dinotopian engineers based the design on marine invertebrates, particularly trilobites, horseshoe crabs, lobsters, and giant isopods.

▶ next page
Intruder

A crab sprog patrols the eastern seaport city of Prosperine, where the Saurian Knights maintain clandestine headquarters. The 8-legged strutters serve on mobile surveillance and detention duty. They can deploy smaller strutters and drones to scout the alleys of the inner marketplace.

# Landis Fields

Mechelangelo

The MB-2 Block 50 stonecutter a.k.a. Mechelangelo is a multiroll terra drone maintained by the United States Air Force. This remote "bunker buster" is dropped from an AC-130 via parachute to assist combatants in gaining access to mountainous hideouts by carving out troublesome terrain and other geographical obstacles in the field. Its modular payload consists of 1 water saw with interchangeable bits and 1 "pieta" pod for ballistic slug seeding when roughing.

LANDIS FIELDS

BLOCK 50 | STONE CUTTER

MB-2

"MECHELANGELO"

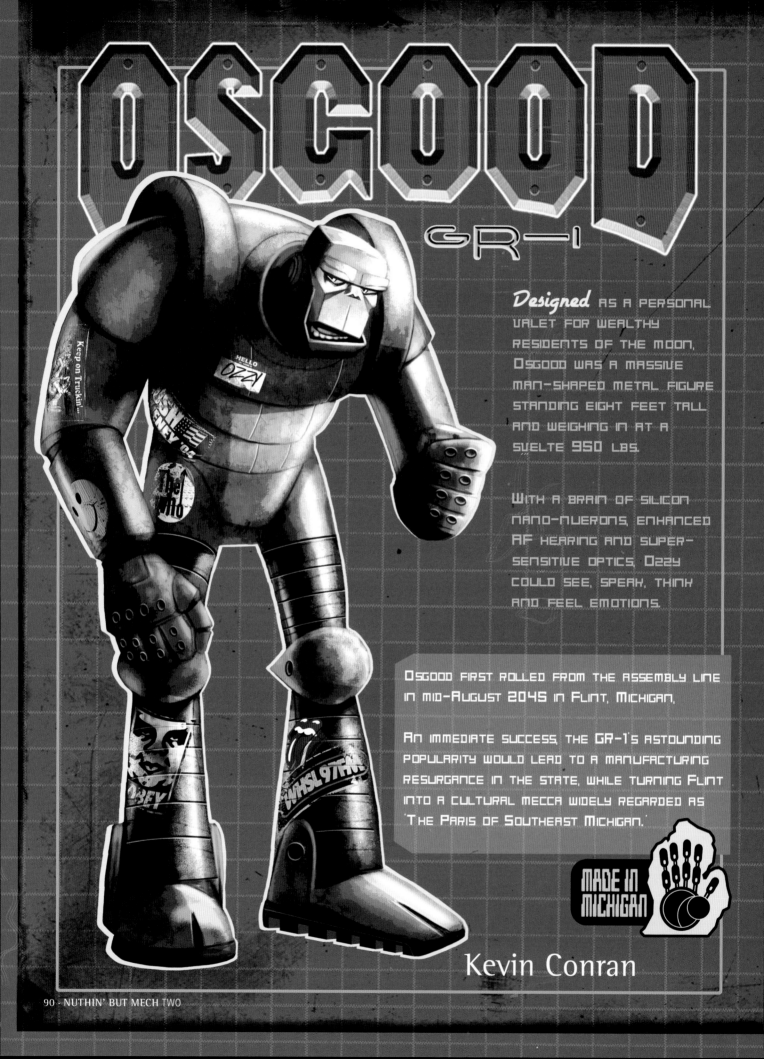

# OSGOOD GR-1

**Designed** as a personal valet for wealthy residents of the moon, Osgood was a massive man-shaped metal figure standing eight feet tall and weighing in at a svelte 950 lbs.

With a brain of silicon nano-nuerons, enhanced AF hearing and super-sensitive optics, Ozzy could see, speak, think and feel emotions.

Osgood first rolled from the assembly line in mid-August 2045 in Flint, Michigan.

An immediate success, the GR-1's astounding popularity would lead to a manufacturing resurgance in the state, while turning Flint into a cultural mecca widely regarded as 'The Paris of Southeast Michigan.'

MADE IN MICHIGAN

Kevin Conran

For all his brawn, Ozzy was a gentle giant, his tremendous strength and stamina powered by the most game changing innovation in the annals of moderne robotics.

The *Hotchiss Multi-System Transformer*, or, as it was better known, the H.M.S.T.R. Engine.

But, as with most good things, it was not to last.

Ironically, it would be the H.M.S.T.R.s ruthless efficiency that would be its undoing.

Virtually indestructable, and possessing a nearly inexhaustable power supply, demand for new Osgood models would grow. In order to answer that demand, an economy model was rerleased in the spring of 2051. The Asgood LS.

In order to keep up with demand and stem runaway manufacturing costs, more and more work was shipped off planet, ultimately leading to massive earthside layoffs and factory closures.

Production of all Osgood lines would end in 2061. However, Osgood can still be found at vintage robot conventions everywhere. Built to last – the H.M.S.T.R. still runs.

James Paick

Jan Urschel

# Lorin Wood

Abstractitron

I wanted to challenge myself to create a piece that was reminiscent of both early-1980s science-fiction magazine art, typically found on *Popular Mechanics* covers, and the early commercial and industrial work of Syd Mead. Rather than stick to a structured composition, I opted to pull a macro shot of something mechanical that really does not warrant any explanation. I also executed this illustration primarily freehand with 4 different digital gouache brushes on a single layer in Photoshop, attempting to capture the imperfection and spontaneity of living with your mistakes. It was a liberating exercise.

MattTkocz

BULLFROG
MOUNTAIN RESCUE

Secondary Gripper

Exhaust

Winch

Rock Climbing Foot

Snow Foot

Primary Gripper

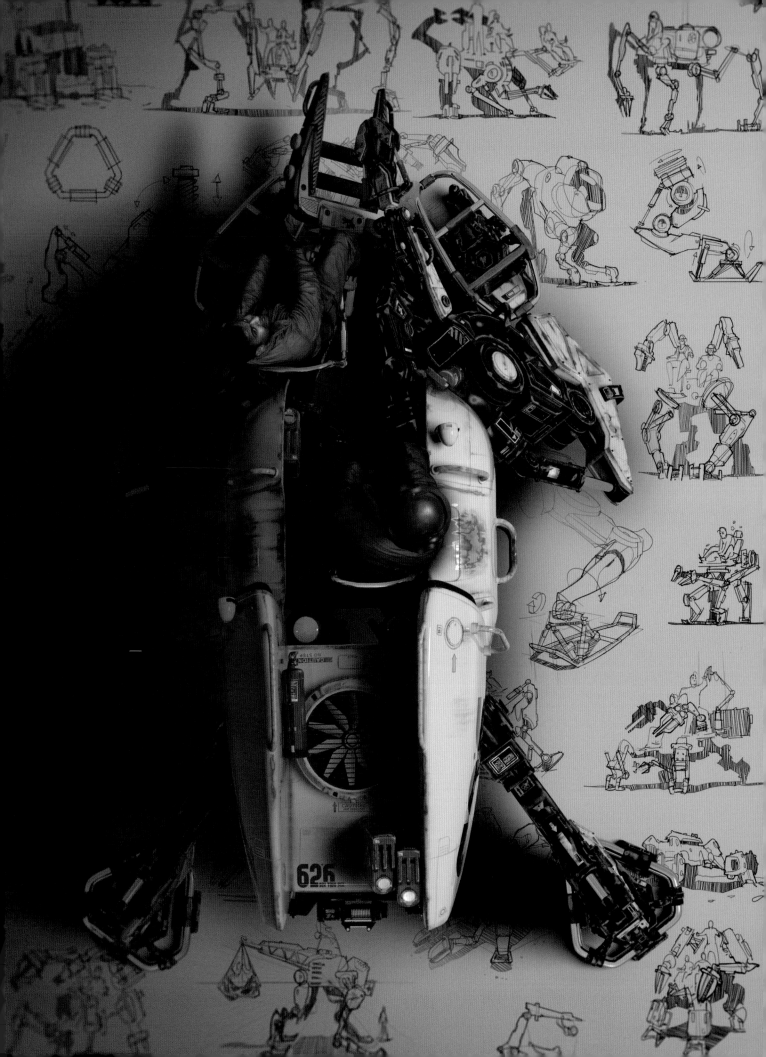

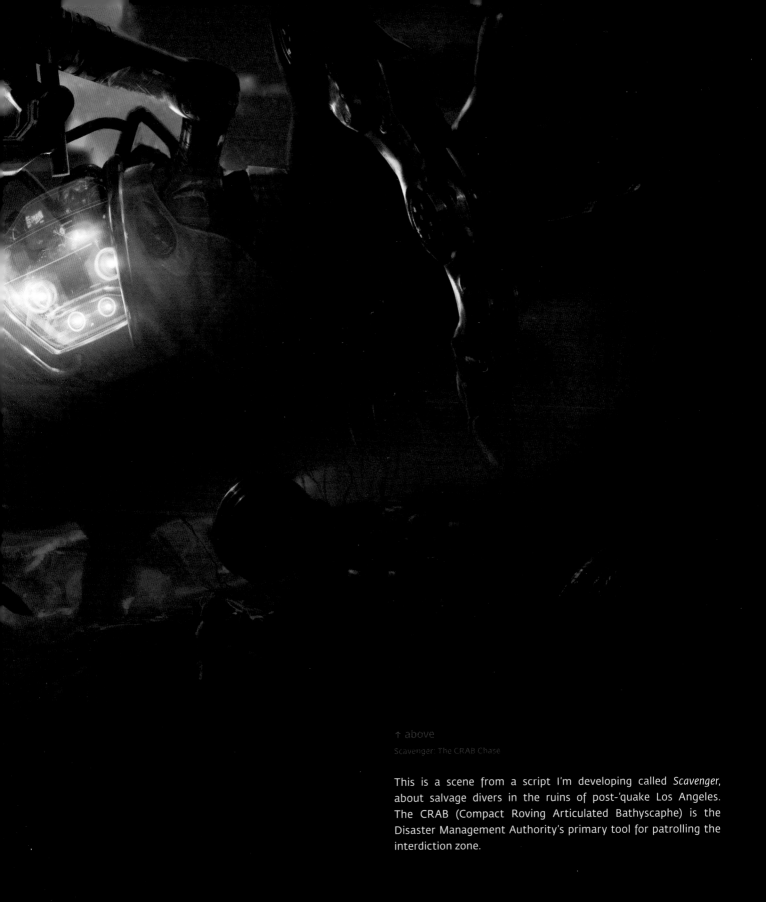

↑ above

Scavenger: The CRAB Chase

This is a scene from a script I'm developing called *Scavenger*, about salvage divers in the ruins of post-'quake Los Angeles. The CRAB (Compact Roving Articulated Bathyscaphe) is the Disaster Management Authority's primary tool for patrolling the interdiction zone.

I've had a fondness for crab tanks ever since *Ghost in the Shell* but never got around to attempting one until now. Unlike the usual massive, lumbering behemoths, I wanted to do something fast and nimble that would skitter sideways like a crab with the turret pointed in the direction it's going. The many legs with minimal contact points would make it ideal for navigating heavily mined terrain. The force of any unavoidable explosion would be deflected by the heavily armored and studded underbelly. I also liked the idea of a very vertical transporter dispensing them into the Drop Zone out of a magazine-like bay.

Robert Simons

RAETORIA

082-B

# Sunil Pant

↑ above

This initially started as a concept for a personal project of mine called 'Mumbai 2050' where this vehicle is to be used as a medical evacuation platform, typically referred to as a 'MED-VAC' in a war zone for wounded soldiers on the battlefield. The vehicle has a chamber in the back that has various life support equipment and a team of highly qualified doctors ready to perform any procedure required no matter the circumstance.

↓ below

This model was created in SKetchUp as a 3D block-out model before the final render (previous page) which was executed in Hypershot. From the front I wanted it to look like a truck, hence the metal frame bumpers with retro fitted headlights.

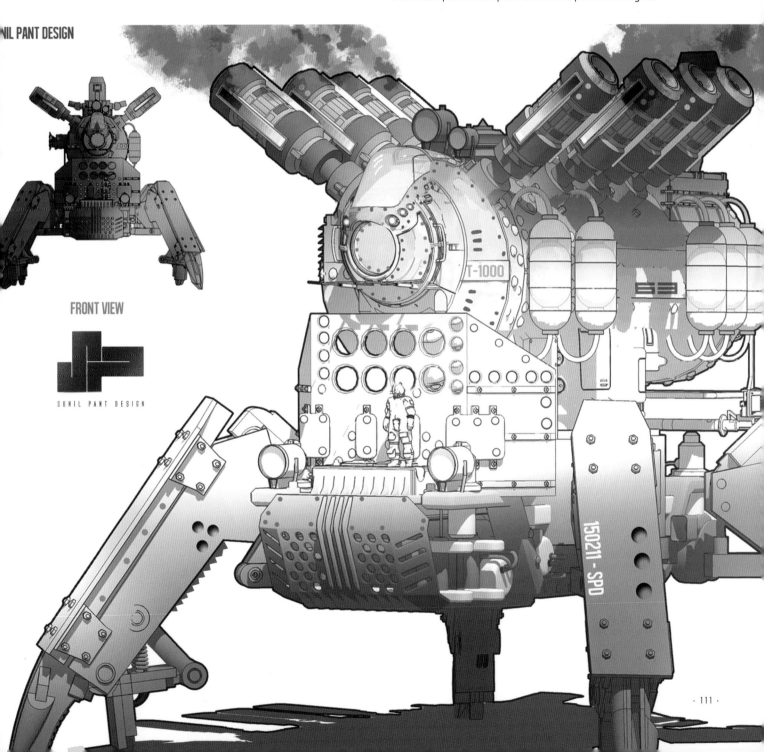

NIL PANT DESIGN

FRONT VIEW

SUNIL PANT DESIGN

MSRX-23 POMBOT

# YUMTEK RHI

VAUGHAN LING
1.2013

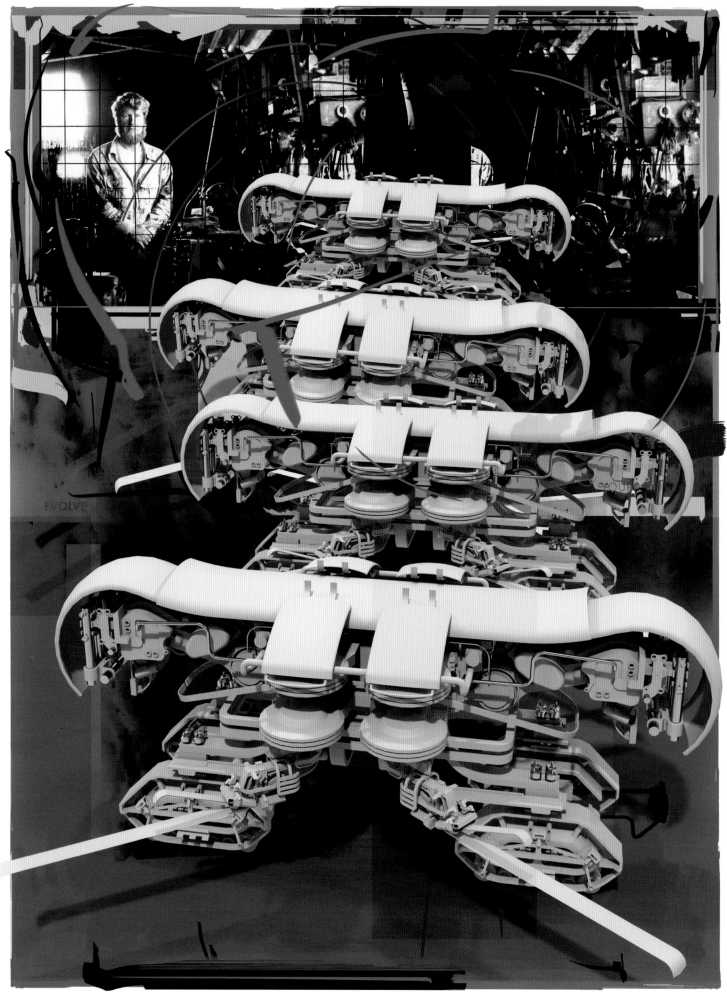

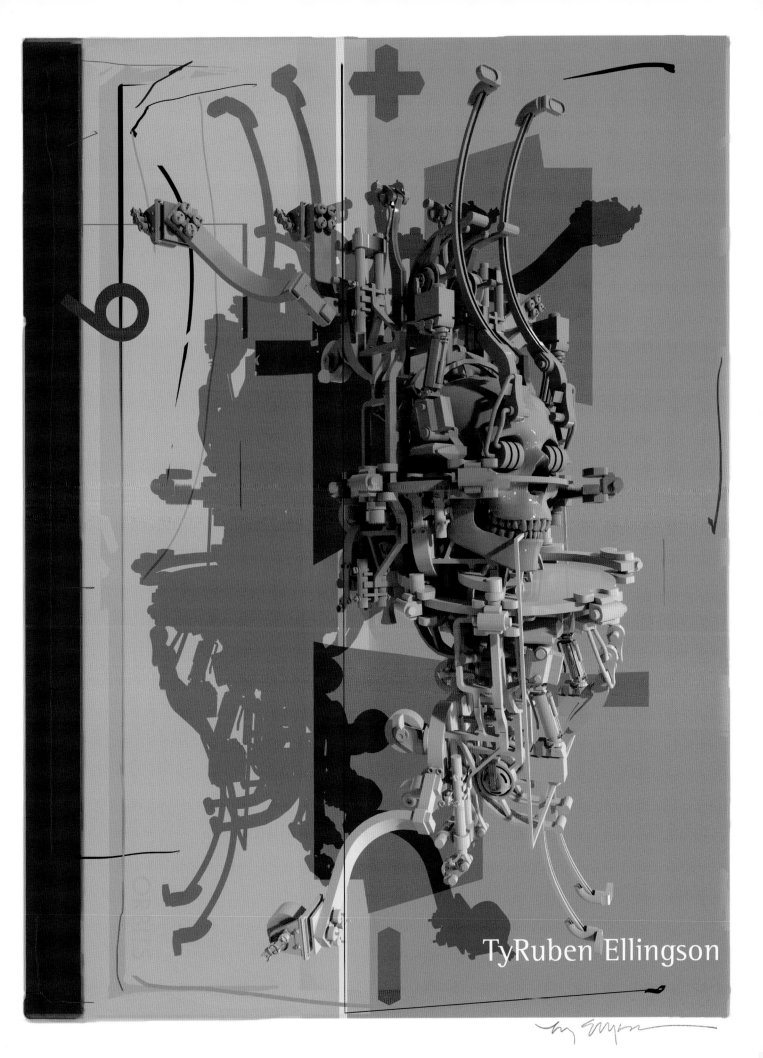

TyRuben Ellingson

## AARON BECK

pgs. 08–09

WEBSITE: www.aaronbeck.com

EMAIL: aaron@aaronbeck.com

Aaron Beck comes equipped with a self-assembling carbon titanium skeleton, carbon nanotube-based electroactive poly-moly muscle units, spider-silk protein skin armor layering with kinetic ablation technology, Wacom-compatible digits, a skull for a face, and a centralized processor unit specializing in advanced use of hexagons. In addition to all that, when tuned to optimum input-output homeostasis performance, he is capable of next-level cock 'n' balls drawings.

## ALEX JAEGER

pgs. 10–13

WEBSITE: alxartblog.blogspot.com

Alex Jaeger studied automotive design at the College for Creative Studies in Detroit and then turned to entertainment design at the Art Institute of Pittsburgh. Soon after graduation, he was working in both the model shop and art department at Industrial Light & Magic. There he has served as a visual-effects art director for more than 18 years on projects such as *Star Trek: First Contact*; *Wild Wild West*; *Starship Troopers*; *Deep Impact*; *Galaxy Quest*; *Pearl Harbor*; *Star Wars: Episodes 2 and 3*; *Transformers 1, 2, and 3*; *Mission: Impossible 1, 3,* and *4*; J. J. Abrams' *Star Trek*; and, most recently, *Pacific Rim*. He is responsible for such designs as the Akira-class starship, Bumblebee's head, the Clone Trooper variations, the future police officer's mask from *Star Trek*, and many others. When he is not art-directing, he is busy being a dad/husband/handyman and drawing cars and, of course, robots.

## ARA KERMANIKIAN

pgs. 14–17

WEBSITE: www.kermaco.com

WEBSITE: www.workshops.cgsociety.org

Ara Kermanikian is a concept designer with a focus on futuristic character, creature, vehicle, and set design. He is also the author of *Introducing Mudbox*, published by Sybex Wiley, and several articles in 3-D magazines. He is currently working on his second book, to be published in 2014 by Design Studio Press. He periodically teaches a polysculpting workshop at CG Society. He holds a bachelor's degree in computer science from California State University, Northridge, and has studied at Art Center and Gnomon School of Visual Effects.

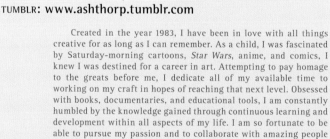

## ASH THORP

pgs. 18–19

WEBSITE: www.ashthorp.com

TUMBLR: www.ashthorp.tumblr.com

Created in the year 1983, I have been in love with all things creative for as long as I can remember. As a child, I was fascinated by Saturday-morning cartoons, *Star Wars*, anime, and comics, I knew I was destined for a career in art. Attempting to pay homage to the greats before me, I dedicate all of my available time to working on my craft in hopes of reaching that next level. Obsessed with books, documentaries, and educational tools, I am constantly humbled by the knowledge gained through continuous learning and development within all aspects of my life. I am so fortunate to be able to pursue my passion and to collaborate with amazing people on feature films and projects.

## BASTIAAN KOCH

pgs. 20-22
WEBSITE: www.marauderfilm.com
IMDB: www.imdb.me/koch

Bastiaan Koch is a Dutch-American film director and writer at the intersection of narrative, design, and digital visual effects. He is a member of Industrial Light & Magic and Marauder Film. Koch is most noted for his work on powered exoskeletons, robotics, and his CG mech design for *Pacific Rim* and the *Transformers* movie franchise. He wrote and produced the film The *3rd Letter*, his screenplay for which was nominated for a 2012 Beverly Hills Film Festival Award.

At age 21, after obtaining a degree in industrial design with a specialization in design for the disabled from Middlesex University in London, Koch helmed Danny Boyle's film *Sunshine* as a designer and model supervisor, working at 3 Mills Studios. He has since worked on more than 6 movies with Lucasfilm in San Francisco. Koch and his team at Marauder Film are focused on developing new narrative-driven films and other commercial film collaborations.

## CALUM ALEXANDER WATT

pgs. 23-25
WEBSITE: www.calumalexanderwatt.com

Calum Alexander Watt is a freelance story boarder, concept artist, and illustrator working in the entertainment industry. He has created artwork for Disney, SEGA, DC Entertainment, and Framestore. He lives and works in the United Kingdom, somewhere near the sea.

## BRIAN HAGAN

pgs. 26-27
http://www.artofhagan.com/

Brian Hagan is an art director, concept artist, and Designer, often shifting from one to the other as a project requires. His overriding passion is to create new and interesting IPs and content that works in a commercial realm but maintains a distinctive fingerprint.

## COLIE WERTZ

pgs. 28-31
WEBSITE: www.coliewertz.com
FACEBOOK: www.facebook.com/ColieWertzDesign

Colie Wertz has been on the VFX side of film for 17 years. An avid sketch artist and CG generalist, his journey began at Industrial Light & Magic at the start of the *Star Wars* prequels. He closed out his run at ILM after *Transformers*, migrating to The Orphanage in an effort to get more mileage on off-the-shelf software. An Art Department invite from ImageMovers Digital enabled him to pursue a VisDev/Concept Design role in both 2-D and 3-D. He is currently a contractor for VFX and concept art and design, and a consultant for a 3-D printing company. Recent projects include vehicle design for *After Earth, Flight,* and *Looper,* including matte painting for *Star Trek: Into Darkness.* His interests include motorcycle/automotive racing and design, reading nonfiction, and the never-ending process of applying learned techniques in design and life.

## DANNY GARDNER

pgs. 32-34
WEBSITE: www.dannydraws.com
WEBSITE: www.formflowforce.com
EMAIL: dannydraws@gmail.com

From the beginning, Danny Gardner has had a passion for art. Born in 1989, he grew up in a family of creative people and designers. He took figure drawing, painting, and animation classes in high school, along with product- and transportation-design classes through Art Center College of Design's Saturday High program. Danny had always dreamed of attending Art Center to major in transportation design. But after a year at Pasadena City College, when he was ready to apply to Art Center, he became aware of entertainment design: it was going to become a new major at school. Having immediately fallen in love with concept design, he changed his focus, though he still has an immense passion for automobiles. After attending Art Center, Danny is now a concept artist in the entertainment industry, working at Sony Santa Monica. He has a rapidly growing interest in painting and product design, and looks forward to producing the ideas in his head through many different artistic outlets.

## CHRIS STOSKI

pgs. 35-37
WEBSITE: www.stoskidigital.com

In his 14 years in the entertainment industry, Chris Stoski has worn many hats. As a concept designer, he has worked on more than 30 exciting Hollywood feature films, several riveting games, one supercool music video, and one Fruit of the Loom underwear commercial. Aside from grown men in tights dressed as giant fruit, he has designed shots for *Star Trek*, *Star Wars*, *Mass Effect III*, *Looper*, VFX Academy Award winner *Hugo*, his wife's yearly birthday cards, and more. He has designed numerous shots and matte paintings for Matte World Digital, and during his years at Industrial Light & Magic he supervised teams on *Iron Man*, *Pirates of the Caribbean III*, and *Star Trek* before moving to Disney and then Doug Chiang Studio. As an art director, Stoski has worked at Atomic Fiction and Digital Domain on *Star Trek: Into Darkness*, *Percy Jackson: Sea of Monsters*, *The Legend of Tembo*, and *Flight*. Stoski loves all genres of design and inventing robots. He really wants a self-driving electric car and prefers hot days to stay below 77 degrees Fahrenheit (that's 25 Celsius to the rest of the world). He currently lives in California, where it's normally nice.

## DARREN BARTLEY

pgs. 38-40
WEBSITE: www.fightpunch.cghub.com
BLOG: fightpunch.blogspot.co.uk
EMAIL: fightpunch@googlemail.com

I was brought onto the planet in 1979; unfortunately, this was too late to see Star Wars in the cinema. I knew this was a mistake, so I made sure I saw *Return of the Jedi* in one at the age of 4. From then on I watched a ridiculous amount of movies and played a ridiculous amount of games. I also drew. At age 18 I developed an obsession with concept art/design that has never gone away. I hope it never does.

## SAM BROWN

pgs. 41-43
BLOG: sambrown36.blogspot.com
WEBSITE: www.sambrown36.carbonmade.com

A senior concept artist at Massive Black in San Francisco, Sam Brown graduated from the University of Cincinnati with a degree in industrial design. He studied product and automotive design. Shortly after finishing school, he began working for Massive Black.

## DAVID HOBBINS

pgs. 44-45
WEBSITE: www.davidhobbins.com
WEBSITE: www.sketchmeta.com

In my childhood, I was a geek for anything shiny that moved—airplanes, cars, rocket ships, you name it. I used to obsessively pore over the art books of Ralph McQuarrie and sketched as many cars and airplanes as I could. After working for a bit in animation, I went to the Art Center College of Design in Pasadena to study transportation design. There, I also pursued entertainment design. From there I was lucky enough to work at Lucasfilm on the live-action *Star Wars* TV show then in development, and then at ImageMovers Digital on various films. I am currently freelancing on a few pitch projects.

## DYLAN COLE

pgs. 46-48
WEBSITE: www.dylancolestudio.com

Dylan Cole is a concept artist, matte painter, and production designer working in the entertainment industry. Since graduating from UCLA in 2001, he has contributed art to more than 60 films. Notable credits include senior matte painter on *Return of the King*, concept art director on *Avatar*, and production designer on *Maleficent*. The Southern California native grew up drawing spaceships and alien worlds; this passion led to the creation of his first book, *The Otherworldly Adventures of Tyler Washburn*. Cole enjoys teaching workshops at various events and schools around the world and has a line of instructional DVDs from the Gnomon Workshop. He lives in Playa del Rey, California, with his wife, Bethany, and son, Adrian. He is currently co-production designer on the Avatar sequels.

## FAUSTO DE MARTINI

pgs. 49-52
BLOG: faustodemartini.blogspot.com
EMAIL: fausto3d@hotmail.com

Fausto De Martini started his career as a freelancer working for advertising companies in Brazil and got a job as a cinematic modeler at Blizzard Entertainment, posting the Image "Marine" on CG Channel and CGTalk. De Martini was part of the production of world-famous cinematics for games such as *World of Warcraft*, *StarCraft 2*, and *Diablo 3*. His most famous piece was the model of the *StarCraft 2* Space Marine Suit, which he helped design; he was responsible for the high-resolution model and mechanical design of the suit assembly parts in the intro cinematic. De Martini recently made a transition from Blizzard to work as a concept illustrator on movies. His first project in the movie world was the remake of *RoboCop*, and he recently worked on *Transformers 4*. Many of his personal works have been featured on book covers, graphic card boxes, and ATI Graphics card advertisements. His work Cosmonaut has been used as the main advertising image for the sculpting software Mudbox.

## JAKE PARKER

pg. 1
WEBSITE: www.mrjakeparker.com

Jake Parker is an illustrator, concept artist, and comic creator. Since the turn of the century, he has worked in the publishing and entertainment industries on everything from commercials and animated films to graphic novels and picture books. His film credits include *Titan A.E.*, *Horton Hears a Who*, *Ice Age 3*, and *Rio*. He is also the creator of the all-ages graphic-novel series *Missile Mouse*, published by Scholastic. He lives in Utah with his wife and children.

## EDDIE DEL RIO

pgs. 54–55

WEBSITE: www.eddiedelrio.com

Eddie Del Rio is a concept artist based in the San Francisco Bay Area. Past clients include LucasArts, THQ, EA, Legendary Pictures, Activision, 2K, Disney, Walt Disney Imagineering, and Lucasfilm. Some of his latest projects include the new *Godzilla* feature film currently in production, *Bioshock Infinite: DLC,* and *XCOM.* Currently, Eddie is busy freelancing for film, games, and TV.

## ELIOTT LILLY

pgs. 56–57

WEBSITE: www.eliottlillyart.com
BLOG: eliottlillyart.blogspot.com

Eliott Johnson Lilly is a freelance concept artist and digital illustrator, currently working in the video game and movie industry. Graduating from the School of Visual Arts (2006) located in New York City, with both his BFA and MFA in illustration, Eliott has been working in the industry for over 7 years. Durring the course of his career, he has helped lead the visual development for several projects, most notably; *F.E.A.R. 3, RAGE* and *DOOM 4.* When he's not drawing robots, or working on a personal project, you may find him learning new things at his desk, spending time with his friends and family, or just playing *Plants vs. Zombies* with his fiancee, Kim.

## EMMANUEL SHIU

pgs. 58–59

BLOG: eshiu.blogspot.com

Emmanuel Shiu currently specializes in concept design/illustration/visual development for the film and video-game industries. He has contributed to a variety of high-profile projects for film (*The Amazing Spider-Man 2, Cloud Atlas, Captain America: The First Avenger, Star Trek: Into Darkness, Looper, Superman Returns, Harry Potter and the Goblet of Fire, Hellboy*) and video games (*Lost Planet 3, Rise to Honor, DroidWorks*).

## JOSH NIZZI

pgs. 60–62

WEBSITE: www.joshnizzi.com

Josh Nizzi graduated from the University of Illinois with a degree in graphic design. He spent the next 9 years working in video games as an art director, concept artist, modeler, and animator. Since then, Nizzi has been a concept illustrator for feature films. He continues to work on video-game projects as well as venturing into toys, comics, television, and theme-park design.

## FRANCIS TSAI

pgs. 63-65

WEBSITE: www.teamgt.com

I am an artist currently living in Austin, Texas. Prior to that I worked as an illustrator and concept artist in San Diego, California. Most of my work has been in the video-games industry, but I have also done work for comic-book publishers, role-playing games, trading-card games, and film and TV design. I have also authored 2 art-instruction books. In 2010, I was diagnosed with ALS, which is a degenerative neuromuscular disease with no known cause or cure. It typically leads to total paralysis and eventually death from respiratory failure. When the disease took my arms and hands, I spent some time learning to paint on my iPhone with my big toe. Eventually even this stopped being an option. With the help of an extremely technically savvy friend I was able to obtain a custom-built computer setup that is controlled via eye gaze. This new system allows me to use tools such as SketchUp and Photoshop to create artwork. The images shown here are some examples of that.

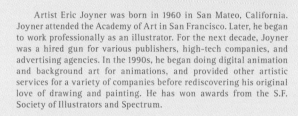

## ERIC JOYNER

pgs. 66-68

WEBSITE: www.ericjoyner.com

Artist Eric Joyner was born in 1960 in San Mateo, California. Joyner attended the Academy of Art in San Francisco. Later, he began to work professionally as an illustrator. For the next decade, Joyner was a hired gun for various publishers, high-tech companies, and advertising agencies. In the 1990s, he began doing digital animation and background art for animations, and provided other artistic services for a variety of companies before rediscovering his original love of drawing and painting. He has won awards from the S.F. Society of Illustrators and Spectrum.

Awards:
1989 Judges award, S.F. Society of Illustrators.
1989 gold medal, unpublished category.
2003 Spectrum Gold medal
2004 Spectrum cover
2004 Honorable mention

## JEREMY COOK

pgs. 69-71
WEBSITE: www.2D2cg.com
EMAIL: Jeremy@2D2cg.com
TWITTER: JeremyCook3D

Jeremy Cook has been a digital artist for more than 17 years. In that time he has been in film, games, and cinematics at houses including Industrial Light & Magic and Blur Studio. He has worked as a modeler, matte painter, and concept artist on projects including *Transformers 1*, *Star Wars Episode 3*, *Mission: Impossible 3*, *The Day After Tomorrow*, *Sucker Punch*, and countless TV commercials, game cinematics, and magazine covers. For the past 5 years, he has been in games, continuing in a diverse career of CG. As a production designer and art director at Microsoft Studios, he works with several game companies to make the games you play look good. When not working, he loves spending time with his family in the beautiful Pacific Northwest city of Kirkland.

## GAVRIIL KLIMOV

pgs. 72-74
WEBSITE: www.hexeract.org
TUMBLR: gavriilklimov.tumblr.com
TUMBLR: hexeract.tumblr.com

Gavriil Afanasyev Klimov is a freelance concept artist in the movie and game industries. Born and raised in Europe, he moved to Los Angeles upon completing high school to attend Art Center College of Design, majoring in industrial design with a focus on entertainment design. His clients include Activision, Adhesive Games, Blizzard Entertainment, Digital Frontier, Ignition Creative, Kojima Productions, MPC, Nike, Paramount Pictures, Pixar Animation Studios, Prologue, Rhythm and Hues, and Treyarch, among others.

## ROBH RUPPEL

pgs. 75-77
BLOG: broadviewgraphics.blogspot.com
EMAIL: robhrr@yahoo.com

Robh Ruppel designs for feature films, theme parks, animation, and video games. He has been nominated for an Annie Award and won Best Art Direction for *Uncharted 2* and *3*. He has also received gold and silver awards from the Spectrum Fantasy Art Annual. When not painting or designing on a commercial project, he can be found working on his own art of adding base miles to his weekly ride average.

## IAN MCQUE

pgs. 78-79
BLOG: mcqueconcept.blogspot.com
EMAIL: ian.mcque@gmail.com

Ian McQue is the assistant art director/lead concept artist at video-game developer Rockstar North, where he is part of the team that creates the *Grand Theft Auto* series. The gritty realism of these games is something that McQue tries to inject into his personal work, striving to create a fantasy world that has a resonance and believability.

## JAMES GURNEY

pgs. 80-85
BLOG: gurneyjourney.blogspot.com

James Gurney comes from a long line of mechanical-engineering ancestors and relatives, starting with Goldsworthy Gurney (1793–1875), builder and popularizer of steam-powered carriages in 1830s England, and Dan Gurney (b. 1931), driver and constructor of race cars. James Gurney spent his childhood scratch-building radio-controlled gliders, model ships, and latex monster masks. He brought these maker instincts to the design of his New York Times best-selling *Dinotopia* book series, which he both wrote and illustrated. He designed the World of Dinosaurs stamps for the U.S. Postal Service and has worked on more than a dozen assignments for *National Geographic* magazine. Solo exhibitions of his artwork have been presented at the Smithsonian Institution, the Norman Rockwell Museum, and the Norton Museum of Art. He has recently been named a Grand Master by Spectrum Fantastic Arts, a Living Master by the Art Renewal Center, and a Mess Master by his wife. His most recent book, *Color and Light: A Guide for the Realist Painter* (2010), has been Amazon's #1 best-selling book on painting for more than 150 weeks and is based on his daily blog, gurneyjourney.blogspot.com.

## LANDIS FIELDS

pgs. 86-89
TUMBLR: www.landisfields.tumblr.com

Landis Fields is an artist/filmmaker in the visual effects, feature animation, television, and video-game industries. Having specialized in multiple phases of production for various projects throughout his career, his portfolio ranges from Super Bowl commercials to *Star Wars*. Fields discovered 3-D during his enlistment in the military, while serving as an F-16 Avionics Specialist in the United States Air Force.

## KEVIN CONRAN

pgs. 90-91
WEBSITE: www.kevinconran.com

Kevin Conran got his first robot at the turn of the 20th century. His name was Rex, and Conran loved that little robot. Constant companions and best pals, the duo shared countless adventures for many years. But one day, Rex would be sent to live on a "nice farm upstate." And though that would be the last Conran would ever see of Rex, he never forgot him. As the years passed, Rex would go on to inspire much of Conran's work. Whether a world of tomorrow for a brave sky captain and his beautiful one-eyed fighter pilot/love interest, or animated worlds of martians and dragons and monsters and bees, Conran's work would go on...as would his memories of Rex. Conran lives in Los Angeles with his wife and 3 kids, and he does a bunch of stuff in film and TV.

## KURT KAUFMAN

pg. 2
WEBSITE: www.kurtkaufman.com

Kurt Kaufman grew up in the Detroit area, eventually making his way west to attend Art Center College of Design in Pasadena, where he graduated with a degree in transportation design. While at Art Center, Kaufman had the good fortune of meeting the artist whose work had most influenced him: Syd Mead. The meeting with Mr. Mead, who was then working on both *Tron* and *Blade Runner*, inspired Kaufman to pursue a career as an artist in the film industry. Kaufman's successful career has included work on more than 15 feature films (among them *Hook, Jurassic Park, Star Wars episodes 1* and *2, War of the Worlds, Polar Express,* and *A Christmas Carol*), as well as video games and theme parks. Kaufman also has a passion for motorcycles, bicycles, and other "gadgets," which served as inspiration for his Multi-Tool Adventure-Bot. Kaufman lives among the vineyards of Sonoma County, California, with his wife and 2 border collies. In his spare time, Kaufman also makes a pretty damned good wine.

## MIGUEL LOPEZ

pgs. 53
WEBSITE: www.devilminer.com
BLOG: devilminercom.blogspot.com
EMAIL: mlopezart@yahoo.com

Miguel Lopez is an El Paso-born artist working as a vehicle/concept designer for Mattel's Matchbox and Hot Wheels teams in El Segundo, California. Since he moved to Los Angeles, Lopez has been hired for work on video games, commercials, movie posters, comic books, and toy lines. He is an Arizona State University graduate in industrial design and still attends workshops and courses in the L.A. area to keep up with today's competition. Lopez's true obsession, however, lies in his hometown visits with family, where he gets to devour the scrumptious drowning flautas at the one and only Chico's Tacos.

## JAMES PAICK

pgs. 92-94
WEBSITE: www.scribblepadstudios.com

James Paick is the founder and creative director at Scribble Pad Studios, founded in 2008. Soon after graduating from Art Center College of Design, Paick went to work for a number of companies and clients in advertising, illustration, and conceptual design. Soon after, Scribble Pad Studios was established and continues to be at the forefront in entertainment design for clients such as Riot Games, Sony, Crystal Dynamics, NCSOFT, Ubisoft, EA, Epic Games, and Wizards of the Coast, just to name a few. Outside of the studio, Paick is passionate about teaching. He has been fortunate enough to travel the world instructing and educating a vast amount of students hungry for knowledge of this industry and his design process. Paick is currently developing numerous unannounced projects and IPs with his incredible team at Scribble Pad Studios.

## JAN URSCHEL

pgs. 95-97
WEBSITE: www.hendrix-design.com
TUMBLR: janurschel.tumblr.com
EMAIL: jan.urschel@gmail.com

Jan Urschel's journey to the concept-design world was a rocky one to say the least. That his career would have something to do with design and art was obvious early on, his schoolbooks being "beautified" with doodles all through high school. A failed attempt to get into the FH Fotodesign in Munich, Germany, resulted in a master's degree in Japanese studies 5 years later. Who would have thought? All throughout his later high school and university years, however, he supported himself as a self-taught graphic designer for various online and marketing agencies. Fast forward to 2010. Having worked as a lead graphic designer for 2 years in Singapore, he finally enrolled in the FZD School of Design to embark on a journey he had dreamed of for years: becoming a concept artist for the entertainment industry. Shortly after graduation, he was hired by the now-defunct LucasArts Singapore studio to work on *Star Wars 1313*, among other projects. He is a published concept artist and illustrator, working for Ubisoft Singapore during the day and on his freelance business by night.

## LORIN WOOD

pgs. 98-99
WEBSITE: www.lorinwood.com

Lorin Wood has been a conceptual designer in the entertainment industry for nearly 2 decades. Having his passion sparked by copying his father's industrial-design portfolio during his formative years, and a steady diet of art by Syd Mead, Ralph McQuarrie, and Joe Johnston, his downfall from a linear career path was assured. Fast forward and Lorin has been pulled into the world of previsualization and preproduction work for films, tv commercials, video games and wrangling the artists for this book.

## MATT TKOCZ

pgs. 100-103
WEBSITE: www.mattmatters.com
EMAIL: matt@mattamatters.com

Born and raised in Europe, Matt Tkocz moved to California in 2008 to study entertainment design at Art Center. After graduating in 2012, he went on to become another Hollywood phony in the motion-picture industry.

## PHIL SAUNDERS

pgs. 104-107
BLOG: philsaunders.blogspot.com

Phil Saunders gets his mech cred from his suit designs for the *Iron Man* and *Avengers* films. Before a decade in feature-film art departments on movies such as *Tron: Legacy, Cowboys & Aliens, Spider-Man 3*, and *Zathura*, Phil was the creative director of Presto Studios, where he oversaw the design of acclaimed titles such as *Myst 3: Exile* and the *Journeyman Project* series. He started his career working on theme-park-ride design, and had a 4-year stint designing cars for Nissan. Saunders lives in the Los Angeles area and divides his creative energy between professional design work and writing and developing his own projects.

## SUNIL PANT

pgs. 110-112
WEBSITE: www.sunilpant.com
EMAIL: pod@sunilpant.com

Sunil Pant is an entertainment designer engaged in 3-D visual development and prop design for films. He has worked as a senior design artist in the film and game industry for more than 8 years. Having acquired a BFA from the Academy of Art University in San Francisco in 2007, he worked on several Hollywood blockbusters, including *Megamind* for DreamWorks Animation Studios, *Escape from Planet Earth* for Rainmaker Entertainment, and (as a 3-D sketch artist) *Iron Man II*, to name a few. Starting off as an intern working at Electronic Arts on *The Simpsons Game*, he subsequently worked on several projects with the industry's leading art directors. His clients include ESPN, Disney, The Weinstein Company, Mattel Toys, and Prana Animation Studios (India). After about a decade picking up tools of the trade while living and working in San Francisco and Vancouver, he returned to Mumbai, India, in March 2012. He continues to pursue his passion for art at Sunil Pant Design, his new studio in Mumbai, where he is currently working as art director on various features produced in India.

## TYRUBEN ELLINGSON

pgs. 116-118
WEBSITE: www.alieninsect.com

The son of Minnesota artist and university professor William John Ellingson (1933–1994), TyRuben spent his childhood in his father's studio drawing, painting, and constructing cardboard "machines." While completing his master's degree at St. Cloud State University in 1981 and '82, Ellingson taught sections of drawing and design and exhibited his paintings in regional and national shows. In 1988, he completed his master of fine arts degree in painting at Southern Methodist University in Dallas, Texas. Combining his fine-art successes with a lifelong interest in film, Ellingson landed a position as visual-effects art director at George Lucas's Industrial Light & Magic in 1989. While at ILM, Ellingson contributed to the creation of groundbreaking special effects for films such as *Jurassic Park*, *Star Wars: A New Hope*, *The Flintstones*, *Casper*, and *Disclosure*. In 1995, Ellingson accepted an invitation from director Guillermo del Toro to act as principal designer of the signature creature for *Mimic*; the film launched his freelance career. In the following decades, Ellingson provided designs for a number of del Toro's films, including *Blade 2*, *Hellboy*, *Hellboy II: The Golden Army*, and *Pacific Rim*. In 2006, Ellingson joined the team at Lightstorm to work as lead vehicle designer for director James Cameron's science-fiction epic, *Avatar*. Other films to which Ellingson has lent his creative talents include *Blade: Trinity*, *Signs*, *Surrogates*, *Priest*, *Battle: Los Angeles*, and *Elysium*. Beginning in the fall of 2013, Ellingson joined the faculty of Virginia Commonwealth University as a professor in the Communications Arts Department where he teaches classes focused on conceptual design.

## ROBERT SIMONS

pgs. 108-109
WEBSITE: www.robertdraws.com
WEBSITE: www.gadget-bot.com
EMAIL: robert@gadget-bot.com

Robert Simons has been working in the film and game industries for the past 5 years. He has recently worked on the films *Ender's Game*, *The Amazing Spider-Man*, *Transformers 4*, and *Heat*. After these experiences, Simons decided to create his own short film, *Momentum*, which he produced under his company, Gadget-Bot, along with co-creators Peggy Chung and Mark Yang. Look out for *Momentum* in 2014 (momentumrally.com).

## VAUGHAN LING

pgs. 113-115
TUMBLR: vaughanling.tumblr.com
BLOG: vaughanling.blogspot.com
EMAIL: vaughanling@gmail.com

Vaughan Ling is a concept designer/modeler based in Los Angeles. He works in the entertainment industry and teaches design and 3-D modeling at the Concept Design Academy in Pasadena. His first exposure to mechs was through the TV series *Patlabor* in elementary school. He filled binders copying and creating variations on the Patlabor mechs. Today, he is pretty much doing the same thing, although he has learned to avoid using lined paper. So, kids: keep drawing in Spanish class—grades don't matter, as long as you pass—and be nice to your mother. May the future of mech design be glorious!

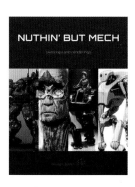
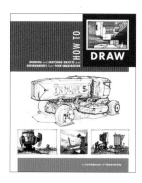